# Limited Atonement

# Limited Atonement

*Poems*

H. C. Kim

## The Hermit Kingdom Press
Cheltenham   Seoul   Bangalore   Cebu City

# Limited Atonement:  Poems

For information address:

The Hermit Kingdom Press
12325 Imperial Highway, Suite 156
Norwalk, California 90650
United States of America
info@TheHermitKingdomPress.com

http://www.TheHermitKingdomPress.com

ISBN:  1-59689-070-3

**Library of Congress Cataloging-in-Publication Data**

Kim, H. C. (Heerak Christian)
  Limited atonement : poems / H.C. Kim.
     p. cm.
  ISBN 1-59689-070-3 (pbk. : alk. paper)
  I. Title.
  PS3611.I4544L56 2007
  811'.6--dc22

                                    2007020351

Dedicated to the Memory of

Dr. Lee, Keun-Sam (d. 2007)

Long-Time Professor of

Korea Theological Seminary (Ko-Shin)

In South Korea

*"The government, which was designed for the people, has got into the hands of the bosses and their employers, the special interests. An invisible empire has been set up above the forms of democracy."*

*President Woodrow Wilson (1856-1924)*

# CONTENTS

# Contents

# Contents

# Preface

Life is about birth, experience, death, and resurrection. Most people are concerned with prolonging their life on earth and making their experiences pleasant as much as possible while living in this world. But you encounter a few who are engrossed by what will happen after the resurrection. This collection of poems explores the stories of both groups of people.

H. C. Kim
Mother's Day, 2007
Palisades Park, New Jersey

# Limited Atonement

## "A Gust of Wind"

A gust of wind
Blew my bag away
Out of the trunk of my car
Like a flash of lightning

And I stood
Watching the bag fly by
Away from the car
Far away from me

Should I chase after it?
I wondered for a second
But it went so fast
And so far away

I knew it would be useless
To chase the bag in flight
Without purpose it flew
But it flew away so fast

A gust of wind
Took the bag right out of my car
I did not even have a second
To grab the bag

So I closed the trunk of my car
And watched the bag fly away
In the cold fall air
Carried by a gust of wind

## "A Puzzled Look"

She threw me a puzzled look
Full of wonder and amazement
There was a search in her face
And it did not find satisfaction

I looked into her face
A blank slate that needed a response
An answer from me
Some kind of expression

I did not knew what to give
For I did not understand the question
So I looked
And presented a blank canvass of my own

And there it was
Two blank canvasses facing each other
Neither wanting to draw on the other
For reasons each did not understand

In the profundity of blank space
Questions suppressed
In the explosion of hidden sentiment
The two canvasses stood

And all receded into the background
Perhaps to be imputed into the mix
Of a masterpiece drawing
To fill the emptiness of the vast canvas

## "Banished"

She found an excuse
To banish him
From her presence

For she could not believe
That he could love her so
She thought herself unlovable

The love he professed frightened her
What if it is genuine?
What if it is not?

She was afraid to get hurt
She had been hurt so many times before
So many professions turned out false

She was there to pick up the pieces
All by herself
Even without the support of "friends"

So she feared
And was overcome by her doubts
And gave her body to someone else

## "Black Bag"

The boy flashed the black bag
And threw it around here and there

He carried the black bag with him
And pushed it in front of him

People were amazed at how beautiful she was
The black bag that he carelessly treated

A young man said
If I were the boy I would treat the black bag better

Another said
The black bag is so beautiful

Others chimed in
The boy doesn't understand its beauty

The boy only uses it like a common bag
But it is a precious, delicate, beautiful bag

People shook their heads
As they saw the boy use and abuse the black bag

The boy did not understand the value
And threw it around like trash

An old lady asked
Why doesn't the boy bring the black bag along?

What? This dirty bag?
The boy replied disrespectfully

The black bag deserves better respect than that
Onlookers observed

Maybe the boy just thinks that bag is inferior
Not worth as much

The boy didn't seem to care
And he threw the black bag into the closet

The boy went merrily along
Planning for his distant travel

With the black bag locked away in the closet
To gather dust like common refuse

People shook their head
How could he not appreciate the black bag?

She's so beautiful
But he can't see her beauty, just her utility

## "Black Pearl"

I asked the boy
Why aren't you taking your black pearl?

The boy replied
He doesn't like the black pearl that much

I was surprised
Because I saw him with the black pearl a few weeks ago

The boy said flippantly
That was just for show and means nothing

It didn't seem right
To use the black pearl and chuck it out

The boy replied
That's life

It doesn't have to be that way
You can bring the precious black pearl along

The boy became irritated
The black pearl is not important!

Of course, it is important
It is a precious gem and loved by many

The boy replied
The black pearl is just to use and abuse

I looked at the boy sadly
For he doesn't understand the value of the black pearl

## "Bonded"

They are bonded by artificial chemical
Substance probably more harmful
Than we are aware
But in the water
With the roll and a tumble

They stick to each other
Like glue bonding delicate paper
Almost inseparable
It's the twists coupled with wetness
That have united them together

Now they lie there entwined
With damp water dripping from the edges
One piece with another
Leg piece with the arm piece
The smell of chemicals still fresh

Pieces of clothing
Bonded like no other bond
At least for this moment
For better or for worse
But in time they will dry

And they will come apart
Tumbling through the dryer
Even the rolled up socks separate
And in the dryness they stand alone
Each piece with no entanglements

And I will pick up the pieces
And throw them in the bag
One that is for such a purpose

Each piece separated
Awaiting to be folded

Soon they will be tucked away
Into the drawers
Of a wooden chest
Awaiting their use once again
And the whole laundry cycle will again begin

**"Carried Off"**

They were carried off
One by one
In the river
Like Moses in the River Nile

Moses was on a little ark
That brought him salvation
Prepared in obedience to God
To protect it from secular power

But the little ones
Drifted on the river
Without a ark
The church never taught about it, really

Unfortunately, without an ark
They drifted bodily on water
Body submerged in deep waters
That carried their bodies to their end

No mercy was there
For they refused the ark
The road to salvation
Christ's protection

The church had become defiled
You see
And the sanctuary was loyal
Less to the Kingdom of Christ

The building could not protect them
Nor the membership in their church
Which they thought belonged to them

They denied the ownership of Christ

The sanctuary was desecrated
Christ's honor runs through the mud
And the little ones
Received the divine wrath

For Christ is a jealous God
Demanding sole worship
Honor, allegiance, and loyalty
The little ones paid for their parents' sins

## "Cleopatra"

How did I become Cleopatra?
Of the ancient lore
She asked herself
While looking in the mirror

For she did destroy men in her path
Not intentionally or out of malice
But with her love
That proved fatal for these men

One fell into it by chance
Out of the sky
Dropped the opportunity
He thought he was the manipulator

Another stumbled into it
By a form of arrangement
So he thought
But he now felt trapped

Yet, another out of youthful fancy
To try something new
Or maybe out of genuine love
He was not sure

All three men
Headed in confusion
Their worlds turned upside down
Each dying in his own way

She looked at herself in the mirror
And did not know what to do
Should I cry or should I laugh?

She continued to brush her hair in hesitation

## "Coach"

You put me in coach
Like I'm your slave
While you sit there in First Class

What do you take me for?
A slave from the slave days
Yessir, master

You put your leg up there
In First Class
And make me cramped down here in coach

What do you think I am?
Your slave
Haven't you heard of emancipation?

Treat me as your equal
Put me up there in First Class
Why should I be treated like your slave?

Don't be sweet talking to me
Trying to persuade me to fly coach
Put some of your other people there

I want First Class
Treat me as your equal
Respect me

## "Condemned"

All saw them
Breaking in and entering
Who are they kidding?
They think they are innocent?

Those in the room saw them
They who had no permission to be there
Others saw them enter in
And they are witnesses against them

The very words they utter
In accusation and in charge
Convicts them conclusively
Of their guilt

They were there!
And they sinned
Consciously
With premeditated precision

They followed the wayward
Making excuses for themselves
Whatever those excuses may be
They are not excuses honored by God

They entered in
Violating the law of the land
Even the Police cannot use evidence obtained
In break-and-entry without warrant

Dignity of the person
Privacy of the individual
These are sacred values

In enlightened democracies

They sought to play God
Like the foolish humans
Building the Tower of Babel
They wanted to reach God's power

They sought to be like God
Like Eve and Adam
Who thought they would know like God
When they ate the forbidden fruit

So, they entered in
To the forbidden place
Where they knew
They should not be

Why did they go in?
Because of the sinfulness of their hearts
Which had become wicked
And they desired to see like God

## "Edinburgh"

I want to be in the middle of it all
Right in the center of the city
To stay in an air-conditioned hotel
Five stars by its side

You can fetch me up there
Or to the town's edge and back
There's a car
And a chauffer can be had

But don't be putting me in the corner
Like a house rat
But put me in the center of it all
Where it's all happening

It's not like I go to Edinburgh every day
It's a special time for me
And make it special for me
Put me in a grand hotel in the city center

Transport me in a carriage
For outings to the outskirts of the town
I don't want no dormitory room
For my stay in the city of kings

Put me in a five star hotel
With first-class service
It's a short stay any way
Make it special

You say this is your town
Why you put me in a dormitory
It's my summer vacation

Put me in a resort hotel

Am I not worth it?
Is not my love of any value to you?
Or were you just lying all the time
With fake earnestness in your eyes?

All your words of affection
Prove them to me
Show me respect
In this city of kings

## "Faux Interviews"

The academics rode in their limousines
And conducted faux interviews
They thought they were in MTV
Maybe they were

They thought they were on a reality show
They never had the spotlight on them
They were nerds all their lives
This is the revenge of the nerds!

The academics wanted to be stars
Even for a day
Or maybe a week
To be wined and dined

They compromised their academic principles
Only ethics they had left
After they renounced religion
And all things organized in society

They still held to what they saw as their dignity
Academic freedom
Respect for the individual
Then they chucked that all out the window

As they rode in their limousines
It felt comfortable to compromise
And sell themselves out
With champagne and caviar

They conducted faux interviews
And made them look real on MTV
Like the interviews after The Survivor

They thought themselves stars

Faux interviews
Meant for TV
Scripted for the producers
Directed by those financing their 30 minutes of fame

## "Fire, Fire"

Fire swept through the wild
They say that an arson started it
Who knows?
Maybe so
Maybe not

Someone could have started a fire
In the wilderness
Just to see how a bush would burn
And imagine Moses before the burning bush
With harmless intention

Deliberate evil?
That's a possibility
Maybe there was an anti-environmentalist
Who wanted to kill all living plant life form
In the desert out in nowhere

The fire did not start in a city
Or even very close to a city
But it spread through the wilderness
And became a great fire
That engulfed 4 firemen in its power

Did a lightning strike
And start a fire
A little spark
That got the fire going?
It's known to have happened before

Fire, fire
Probably more than a few shouted
Especially as the wildfire

Enters the realm of the domestic bliss
Edging closer toward Palm Springs

How the elderly must have fretted
Lest the fire reach their retirement homes
Nothing ever happens here
Just the warmth and sunshine
Maybe a snowfall in a blue, blue moon

The fire spread
And killed the seasoned firemen
Cooked to a crisp
Like deep-fried chicken
Now, buried deep in the earth

**"Firemen"**

The firemen of that city
With the newly elected
The first among firsts
They say so it is
Pondered their fate

What will be?
Should we remain
And the fire consume
The inhabitants
Our family and friends?

No, they said
We are men of action
We are firefighters
We will fight the evil
Conflagration spreading

They each took up the hose
Which can fire the water
Like a speeding bullet
To strike dead
The evil spread

Each vowing their own life
As an assurance
To bring deliverance
Life for life
Death for death

Elected we are
The first of our city
To fight this wicked

Cancerous plague spreading
Throughout the city of our childhood

## "George"

They call him George
Because he is mad
Like the madness of King George

They call him George
Because he's such a riot
He makes everyone laugh

They call him George
Because he kinda look like
The Commander in Chief

They call him George
Because he has leadership
Like that Washington fellow

They call him George
Because he likes to ape
Like that monkey on the screen

They call him George
Because he's a regular guy
Okay, maybe not

They call him George
Because it sounds like
A fire fighter's name

They call him George
Because he's dead as George
Most famous ones any how

They call him George

Because he's a picture on a wall
To remind them of caution

## "Gun Man"

He was a gunman
From the city of the Queen
Who had an obligation
For he volunteered his service
To the Kingdom of Christ
To fight and defend
The Honor of Christ

He was a gunman
The best shot in his class
He knew how to kill
With a sharp shooting skill
He could meet his targets
The number demanded of him
He was skilled and able

He was a gunman
Not wise but foolish
For he threw away his talent
And did not shoot to kill
As he was ordered
And had to do
He believed the wrong people

He was a gunman
Now shot dead
With his wife
And his children
In a robbery unexpected
Who would have known
He would be slaughtered in his sleep?

He was a gunman

Whose memory is a passing fad
Whose life held no real meaning
He didn't live long enough
His children died before they knew
What the world was
His lovely wife dead too

He was a gunman
Who could have made captain
And could have been the pride of his city
The church and in Christ's grace
But he died in disgrace
And is now in Hell
Suffering eternal damnation

## "He Sat There"

He sat there
In front of her
And wondered
What if

What if
It were she
Whom he truly loved
Rather than the substitute

That his cowardice
Has wrought
To face him
As a mirror of his shame

And he partook of the appetizer
That reminded him
That a meal of escape
Had started

And it felt bitter
Even though doused with sweets
Spices and fragrances
And he could only see the ugliness

Of who he was
Sitting there
In front of the one
Who was the substitute for his love

## "I'm Worth It"

I'm worth it
All of me
Every bit of my sweet being

I'm worth it
For the five star treatment
In the streets of London

Don't put me in a dump
There's a five star hotel just down the street
I'm worth it

You driving around in a hummer
BMW
And limousine

Don't tell me
You can't afford it
Or that I'm not worth it

I know both to be untrue
Lies, lies, lies
You know what I mean

I'm worth it
All of me
Every bit of my sweet being

For the five star treatment
Put me in that five star place
Just down the street

It's only a short walk

From this little dump
You've put me in

I know I'm worth it
All of me
And all of my sweet presence

**"Jesus' Visit"**

When Jesus comes back
Everyone will see Him
And know He's God

Sure, the preacher responded
Everybody and every creation will know
They will see and hear

Then the people will all believe
They will believe Jesus is the Only Way
Only God of the Universe

Sure, the preacher responded
Everybody will believe
They will see His glory

Then all will be saved
Because all believe
Jesus is the Only Savior

No, the preacher responded
When Jesus returns
It's too late

What do you mean
Too late
It's never too late for atonement

No, the preacher responded
Limited Atonement in effect
Only for those who believed before His return

## "Judgment"

Judgment fell like a dark sky
Filled with lightning and thunder
Upon a city
Recalcitrant
As to support the anti-Christ
And his mighty network
As men in sheepskin
Bowed and brought Frankincense
As the cloaked ones
Kowtowed and carried Myrrh
The commerce world
Bending and submitted God
Baby Jesus?
What baby Jesus?
The three dumb groups
Coming together
Like sheep before the slaughter
And the gavel fell
Death came upon that city
Judgment of God
Limited Atonement

## "Knocking at the Door"

I heard a knock on my door
And imagined for a second
That the Angel of Death hath come
To claim the marked one

No, not me
My lovely daughter
The apple of my eye
The reason for my toil

She delights me with her smile
She has my eyes
My chin
And my ears

I work and work
Thinking of the joy
She will bring
The moment I return home

I would give my life for her
And everything that is mine
She is my joy
My hope

I heard a knock on the door
And I thought it was a knock next door
The Angel of Death has gone there
To my partner's home

At least for today
The end to my life is passed
My daughter will live

I await fearfully for the knock

That will open the door
To my house and to my family
For the Angel of Death to enter
To claim my daughter who is my life

## "Laundry"

Spinning and spinning
I can see my laundry
Through the circle
Window of the machine

Soap and water
Mixing
Bumping together
Socks and shirts

Mercilessly
The cycle
Repeats
Like an endless circle

And there it is
40 minutes of spin
Spun out
And my clothes washed

Ready for the dryer
Wet through
My clothes await
My collection

I look at the bundle
Bonded in water
Now presumed clean
Just waiting the final dry

## "Life Out"

Life was taken out
For he hesitated
And he beheld his child
Stricken dead
By the Angel of Death

Why did he wait?
He thought
Through the tears
And the dread
Of missing the one in his arms

His child was dead
Struck dead
By the Angel of Death
The priest warned him
Through veiled language

But he did not understand
He did not know
He did not believe
All he had to do is to obey
God's demand of him

He held his dead child
And knew that he died
Because of his sins
His sins of refusing God service
Of disobedience to God

Sin it is
When one disobeys
A direct order from God

Kingdom of God
Held him responsible

The dead child lay in his arms
Still he did not understand
Or refused to understand
He was stubborn in his ways
And thought he could oppose God

He sat there
Watching his other child
Finding comfort
In misplaced hope
For tomorrow she too will die

## "Limited Blood"

Christ's blood shed
To effectuate salvation
Limited by free will
By God's divine decision

Those who will freely choose
To follow Christ
To be born again in His righteousness
To be declared just in His Name

For them
With their free will
Was the blood of Jesus shed
None went to waste

The blood of Jesus
Was not shed for the world
Every single human being
Even those who don't want it

Christ's blood was shed
Only for those
Who would freely receive Him
Out of their own will and decision

Jesus Christ's blood was not wasted
Or thrown on those who do not want it
There is limited blood
Limited by human free will

That's the way God planned it
God offers salvation
But it is human free will to accept

By the grace that is effectual

Christ's blood is not worthless
It is not thrown away
It is reserved
For all who would receive him as God

Jesus's blood shed
Brings salvations to all
Limited only by the decision to accept him
In the effectual grace of our LORD

Limited atonement
Limited blood
Limited salvation
Free will effectuated by grace

## "Lobster in My Oven"

There's a lobster in my oven
I just bought it alive from the Vietnamese market
Five minutes from here

375 degrees
Nice and warm
I can still hear it kicking

Its two claws tied
With a yellow tape
Its little legs moving this way and that

It's in a low lying pan
With iron bars to hold him still
There it is all warming up

I couldn't fit it in a stove
The biggest pot I had
Only barely fit its head

Thank God for the oven
And the long baking pan
In a short while I will be eating this 6-pund critter

The last time I had lobster this big
Was in Main with my dad and mom
And two sisters

And none of us could finish the big lobster
This time I will sure give it my go
And redeem myself for last time culinary defeat

The lobster stopped kicking

Maybe the gas stove gassed it dead
Soon it will be cooked

I will have my fill
Of fresh 6-pound lobster
Picked out from the local Vietnamese market

## "Lobster in the Tank"

My dear little lobster
Do you want to know
Why I have chosen you?

I saw you in the tank
Bubbling with water
In the Vietnamese market

And I knew you were the one
Okay, I will be honest
I did not choose you first

I picked out this big lobster
And thought it was too big
So I dumped it back into the tank

Then I grabbed you by the back
But my eyes deceived me
You were bigger than the first

But I said to myself
Heck, this lobster looks good to eat
And I can handle its size

My dear little lobster
You were chosen
Because I knew somehow you were the one

And I will enjoy eating you
Your tail, claws, your legs and all
With butter and herbs and spices

## "Lobster on Gas"


What must you be thinking?
My little lobster
As you are gassed to death
Inside my little oven

I can only think about how
You would taste in my mouth
Your tender body
Satisfying my every taste bud

But you must be thinking
About something altogether different
Being gassed inside my little oven
Are you high yet?

Gas death gives you a high
For a few moments at least
I can hear you kicking
So you must not be too high on gas

I wonder how long it will take
For the lobster to die
I would measure your time to death
But my oven has no fancy window

But it doesn't really matter to you I guess
I suppose you rather die in darkness
Rather than light shining down on your agony
In a fancy oven with a window to look in

Lobster on gas
That's who you are
And soon you will be a dead lobster

Cooked and ready to eat

**"Love"**

Honey, you love me?
Yes
Then, why didn't you rescue me?
Rescue you?

Yes, you know the prophecy
The prophecy?
Yes, the prophecy, the one
That's just baloney

You love them more than me?
You know you are the world to me
Then, why don't you follow the prophecy?
I don't believe

I don't either, honey
Then, what's all this business
What if it comes true?
It won't

Can you be sure of that?
I guarantee you on my life
Can you guarantee it on my life?
I don't want to

Can you live without me?
You know I can't
Then, follow the prophecy
You know I can't do that dear

Do you love me?
You know I love you more than anything
Then follow the prophecy

Yes, dear

## "Mama Raised No Fool"

Don't be insulting my mama
Mama raised no fool
What do you take my mama for?

You can't put me in there
With a bunch of other people
This ain't no animal pen

I am a glorious human being
Whom mama raised to be smart
Who knows she's all that and more

Don't be insulting my mama
And put me in there with a bunch of strangers
I want my own room

Ain't too much to ask, is it?
I have my own room at home
You have your own room

Why can't I have my own room here?
And take away all the stress
Give me some space for my beauty

Don't be dissing my mama
Mama raised no fool
I am a delectable beauty

I need my beauty sleep
Can't get it being penned in like an animal
I want my own room

Ain't asking much

For a rich person like you
Give respect to mama

Mama raised no fool
She taught me to be smart
And take what I am worth

I'm worth all that and more
Mama raised no fool
I know what I am worth

## "Means Nothing"

Christ's cross means nothing
To those who don't believe
Calling Jesus Christ a man
There is no salvation

There is limited atonement
Only for those who believe
Freely choose to put their faith
In Christ
God and Savior

The rest of the world
Will not be atoned for
For whosoever believes
Shall be saved
Out of already condemned position

Christ's cross means nothing
To those who refuse to repent
Of their sins and their evil ways
Turning away from sin to God
There is limited atonement

God did not become Incarnate
To throw away the Incarnate Blood
For nothing
It is limited atonement
Only for those who freely believe

Christ's cross does not mean nothing
It is of value
And infinite worth
A source of eternal life

And salvation from sin

## "Misses"

Misses rather than hits
When the strike was thrown
And the bat was swung
Correctly to hit a homerun
But the ball was a mere apparition

The ball was thrown
The apparition seen
Again and again
The bat swung yet again
Yet the misguided direction became reality

The bat was real
And the boy knew
Because he could see, feel,
And hear the swing of the bat
He thought the ball was real too

But the ball that he swung after
Passed through his bat
And his swings were useless
Because the real ball was thrown elsewhere
He did not know where

He believed
And searched
For the place of the real ball
Where his perfect swing
Would hit one out of the ballpark

## "Mystery"

She realized the mystery
Which had eluded her
So many times in the past
Of a paradox that was her life

Safety is insecurity
Happiness is sorrow
Celebration is isolation
Acceptance is refusal

She wondered then
In her state of enlightenment
How she was deep in the mire of it
Understanding but helpless

And she understood the mystery
She for many years had sought
The key to her happiness
She was that key

But she felt the paradox
That she the key could not herself turn
Someone has to turn the key
That is she

And she wondered who will help her
To unlock the mystery of her life
And her true happiness
And found that there was none there

Will the key stay inert?
Stuck in the keyhole
Just to be turned

To open the lock

Happiness so close
Yet so stuck
And in effect
Impossible to access

## "No Blame in Love"

There is no blame in love
Pure and divine
Strong and stern
Withstanding all storms
Winds, toils, and aches
Longings, desires, and passions

There is no blame in love
Preserved
Like strawberry jam
On a cold winter day
With a snow blizzard outside
Smell of strawberry pervading the room

There is no blame of love
Given
Freely
No regrets
A gift
Sacred

**"No Rescue"**

There is no rescue
The terminally ill realized
I will die
And that is my lot

There is no rescue
Because rescuers are dead
They are themselves killed
Through the plague

There is death everywhere
Miles and miles
Cities after cities
Limited atonement

Not all will be atoned for
Not everyone will be saved
Most will die with guilt
And enter into Hades

There is no rescue
Because I rejected it
Maybe not pro-actively
But certainly through silence

There is no rescue
I realize that I am guilty
Because I participated in the evil
To push the last rescuer away

## "Noah"

Noah sat there
In his worn down armchair
Exhausted after a bout
Of shouting and screaming

The Flood is coming!
The Flood is coming!
People laughed and hissed
Some turned their heads and ignored him

Outside there was still laughter
Some lads followed Noah home
Just to tease him more
You crazy nut!

Noah sighed as he sat
Hearing the jibes
Some barely audible
Others, loud and clear

He knew the Flood was coming
For God told him so
But no one believed
Try as he might to convince them

Not a single soul
Thought the Flood was coming
Even the religious people doubted
And refused to help build the Ark

Noah has been toiling for years
To build the Ark which God demanded
He shouted as he built

Tried to persuade and cajole

Not he was just worn out
With all the shouting and screaming
All the Ark building
And advertising of the Flood

People outside did not care
They could not believe
That the Flood was coming
To destroy them all

It was so sunny outside
And who's heard of a flood
That can wipe out humanity
What ridiculous non-sense!

God talked to Noah?
Yeah, right?
Who's going to believe that?
They told themselves

Noah built his ark
Day after day
Month after month
Year after year

People got used to his building
Screaming and shouting
Still they could not believe
The message they heard over and over again

Noah sat in his armchair
And wondered how they would sound
As they drowned in the Flood
Children, disabled, elderly

Mothers, daughters, wives
Sisters, brothers, cousins
All shouting in the flood
As they drowned under water

Noah looked into the white wall
And wondered what it would be like
The world covered in rain
Nothing but rain to see

Noah could feel his sore muscles
All the labor to build the Ark
He could feel his throat hurt
All that shouting and screaming

Strangely, he felt peace
As he could imagine the death cries
Of the future from all he knew
Because he did his part

Slowly sleep overtook Noah
Tired and worn out
Rejected by friends and neighbors
And he fell into a loud snore

## "Ode to My Dying Lobster"

How does it feel?
To be gassed inside my little stove
It was brand new when I moved in here
But it's small like the size of my little apartment

You are a happening lobster, aren't you?
Kicking and you would scream if you could
It must be hot as blazes in there
And you can't even see the fire

Nothing like you have ever felt before, eh?
Swimming in the vast ocean
Captured by lobster capturers
Then, put into the water tank

I saw you swimming around
In that tank in the Vietnamese market
It must have been uncomfortable
Your claws tied up in yellow tape

All the lobsters on top of each other
But your legs were moving
Getting their daily exercise
And you did not look too unhappy

I could swear I saw a little smile
And a glitter in your black eyes
When I swooped you up with my hand
From that bubbling water tank

Little did you know
That today was the day of your death
But you have lived a good life

And you are dying an honorable death

Lobsters are meant to die
Eaten by a sea creature
Of a human being
On ground after capture from sea

You have come to your destiny
And you have met the latter
You flew on the plane
How many dead lobsters can say that?

Okay, maybe you didn't fly
Maybe you were transported by a truck
From Maine to California
How many lobsters can say they rode across the US of A?

You have lived a fine life
I am sure
Better than most lobsters
And you have grown a full size

I will enjoy my every bite
Little dying lobster
If that's any consolation
With butter and the whole shebang!

## "Out of Touch"

How can a government be so out of touch?
With things of God that matter
Is the human life the highest value in God's eyes?
Obviously, you haven't read the Book of Joshua
Where God supports annihilation of peoples

Are Muslims enemies of God?
Obviously, you haven't read the Book of Jeremiah
Where God raises up an unbelieving nation of Babylon
And anoints the non-believing King of Babylon
To destroy Israel and the Jerusalem Temple

Who is God's friend?
Who is God's family member?
Christ taught
Family members are those who do the will of God
How can a government be so out of touch?

If the value of human life was the highest value,
God would not have blessed the King of present-day Iran
To decimate the Jewish population
Kill women, children, elderly, and the disabled
The Bible teaches that he was Yahweh's chosen servant

If the Jerusalem Temple was the most important
God would not have allowed the King of Iranians
To destroy the Jerusalem Temple
And kill its priests and teachers of the law
The Bible teaches that this was the will of Yahweh

Who is God's friend?
Who is God's family member?
Christ taught

Family members are those who do the will of God
How can a government be so out of touch?

## "Resigned"

Resigned she was to the forces around her
Feeling helpless like a newborn babe
But with the cognition that revealed
The very helplessness of where she was

What was to be?
What could be?
What has to be?
She asked aimlessly

One side of her
In the remote recesses of her heart
She felt a prick
Of a bitter hope that has gone sour

And she felt the pain immaterial
More poignantly than when she fell
And scraped her knee
Against the harsh pavement of her youth

She wondered if it were true
That time will heal all wounds
And the pain in her heart
Hope that had remained and refused to leave

## "Righteous"

They thought themselves righteous
After breaking and entering
Invading the privacy
With no permission

Regarding his human dignity
Right to private space
They pontificated
From their seats

They not only broke the laws of the Land
They had violated human rights
And humanistic ethnics
They swear by

They broke in
Entered
Violated
Personhood

And they had the gall
To think themselves innocent
They actually thought that they had the right
To call themselves righteous

No
They are criminals
Having broken the law of the land
And they have no respect for human rights

By witnessing the abuse
And doing nothing to stop
Violation after the break-and-enter

They have become accomplices to the wicked deeds

They are not righteous
In the eyes of the law
Humanistic ethics
Or the Law of God

H. C. Kim


## "Ringing Bell"


The bell of the church rang
And called for Holy War
The melodious music
So gentle and so kind
Called for the purification of the land

Why have you defiled my church?
Demanded the LORD
Why have you let them in?
To bring their corruption
And their anti-Christian beliefs

The clergy cowered
For they knew that they did wrong
But gained courage
At the loving second chance
To purify God's church

The normal people of the church
All banded together
To drive out of the church
The Judaizers and the Pharisees
Like in the days of St. Paul

They were going to give Christ sacrifice
The blood to purify the church
The blood of the lamb demanded by God
The blood they were going to put on their doorpost
For the protection of the Triune God

Blood will purify
They knew that
Blood was needed

So they banded together
To collect the blood of the Passover

## "Rolling Fire"

Fire rolled down the forest
Gathered momentum
Rolled still further
Down toward the towns
Engulfing house after house
Fire traveled through the highway
Across the streets
As people evacuated their homes
Asking the cause for God's wrath
That banished them
From the home of their youth
Their lovely neighborhood
Unrecognizable
Amidst the ashes and the smoke
Why?
Rolling Fire

## "Rope"

Noah, throw us a rope!
We are all drowning down here!
Noah saw a family drifting on the sea
Created by sudden rains
Flash floods that came from nowhere

Safely in his Ark
Noah saw them
A whole family
Trying to survive
And felt he should feel pity for them

But he did not
He had told them this was coming
For days and days
Months and months
Years and years

He had given them the message from God
They should build the ark together
Seriously, the amount of help needed as peanuts
In relative terms
And the family would have been saved

They could have obeyed God together
Built the Ark together
Upheld the Kingship of God
And then when the rains came
They would be delivered together

But, no, they refused
To the very day
The Day of the LORD

When the rains started to come
The day the Ark was closed

Noah looked out from the safety of the Ark
And saw a whole family drowning
He knew them all by name
They were next door neighbors
The father was his best friend

Noah, man, open the Ark for us
Throw us a rope
I could see the long rope at the side of the Ark
Why don't you save us?
Have you no heart?

Noah looked at them
And could not feel pity
Maybe it's because of what God said
On the Day of the LORD
You are to praise God's Name

The LORD is King
And He reigns over all
Even nature obeys Him
Don't sour the Day of the LORD
With anything but praise for God

Noah had been prepared
As a believer for this day
The Day of the Judgement for unbelievers
The Day of the LORD to praise
God of the believers

Noah, my son just went under
He's probably dead
He's only five you know

Throw us a rope
So you can save the rest of us

Noah looked at them
Right beneath the Ark
He knew he could save them
He just needed to throw down the rope
They were so close

But the Ark door was closed
The Day of Salvation is over for them
They had to believe before the rain
They had to help the Ark building before the storm
Once the rains came, it was too late

Limited Atonement was in effect
Salvation was closed forever
All outside of the Ark would die
And no help was to be given
Because the Ark was not built for them

The Ark was built for those who believed
Those who put their faith in God
Willingly participating in the building of the Ark
Salvation was possible only before the storm
Before the Day of the LORD

Now, it was too late
Sure, Noah could throw down the rope
And save his neighbors
Drowning and dying before his very eyes
Right within a couple feet of him

But he was not allowed
By the rules of Limited Atonement
Salvation was in effect

Only up until the Day of Judgement
The Ark was built for the repentant

Maybe some repented
You can do a lot of things
When you are actually dying
Who knows if their repentance is real?
It doesn't matter anyway

Even if they are truly sorry
Even if they truly believe
The Ark door is closed
It will not be opened again
All outside are to die

That is the rule of God
Noah knew very well
The story of Lot's wife
She turned back
And was turned into a stone pillar

God can kill those whom He saves
If they disobey His command
In the process of His salvation
Lot's wife turned back outside the city
And was killed by becoming a salt pillar

The Judgment did not kill her
God Himself did
And Noah was not going to experience that
The Ark was closed
No one is to be rescued

The Day of the LORD hath come
For believers to celebrate Divine Visitation
For those who rejected God's Ark

To suffer and die with no salvation
Salvation was limited to those already inside the Ark

Noah shook his head
Trying to muster up a pity-face
A last gift he could give
To his best friend on earth
As he drew his last breaths near the rope

## "Rudolf's Red Nose"

I looked at Rudolf's red nose
Bright and shiny
Made to stand out
On a cloth picture
Of the Christmas joy-animal
And wondered
Why the nose was so red
Was it really to brighten the sky?
Or to testify to the sadness
Beyond the Christmas smile
That there is something
Beyond the visible
A deep longing
A suffering
Covered by the brightness
Of the redness
That is Rudolf's nose

## "Sabotage"

Out of the blue
She sabotaged herself
People wondered
Why?

People talked
Guys tried the male view
Gals sought the female view
But all were perplexed

It's fate!
Some claimed
Others just shook their head
In amazement

It was the talk of the town
The small world
In which they found themselves
They became the spotlight

Who could have thought?
Certainly not the guy in waiting
Thinking that she was in his bag
She surprised him beyond his wildest fantasy

Who knows why she sabotaged herself?
In the manner that she did
Was it an act of protest?
The box she thought she was being cast into

Perhaps she longed for her true love
Who she felt was beyond reach
Love creates desperation

And irrationality

Hope can be dashed
Even with the smallest things
A slight that is minimal or imagined
Becomes a trauma to one in love

Maybe she responded
In desperation
Wanting to hold onto it
That which she desired the most

## "She Sat There"

She sat there
And knew not what to think
For he looked at her
In such a peculiar way

Was it love?
Was it curiosity?
Was it something else altogether?
Did it matter?

She wondered
About herself
About him
And the meaning of life

Is there really love?
And what does it mean?
Where does it come from?
Can it stay forever?

There were just so many things
In this world all around her
That stripped her of her ideal
Romance and love she held dear

And she felt
Innocence lost
As she partook of the appetizer
That suddenly turned sour

H. C. Kim

## "Smell of a Cooked Lobster"

I can smell my lobster
Already cooked in my oven
It was only thirty minutes ago
It was kicking through the yellow tape binding its claws

Soon, I will be sinking my teeth into it
It's tail, claws, legs, and all
With butter, herbs, and spices

I can smell the lobster cooked in my oven
A fishy smell combined with the smell of the sea
A dash of leaked gas and the heat of the oven

In thirty minutes
The lobster became ready
To be eaten, consumed, and digested

It was alive just a few minutes ago
Thirty minutes ago to be exact
Its antennae kept moving this way and that

When I heard it kick and move in the oven
I hoped that the antennae did not catch fire
On the pilot light on the gas oven

Guess it did not
No fire coming out of the oven
Just the sweet smell of a well-cooked lobster

## "Tears"

The little child cried in his father's arms
As she lay there dying
From a rare illness
That the family never heard about

Who knew that their child would be one
In a 100 million who would get this disease
And die a painful death?
Symptoms too much to count

The little child lay there dying
Still believing in the Santa Claus
And the mysteries of life
Abandoned by her tough NYPD dad

The hero of her life
The savior of the innocent
Crusader of justice
Stood there trying to be strong

The little child cried in his father's arms
And asked him
Do you believe in the prophecy, dad?
No, I don't.

Why don't you?
I do.
And the prophecy has come true.
You know the prophecy.

Even as his child lay there in his arms
Dying a death way before his time
He could not believe in the prophecy

He couldn't bear to in the twelfth hour

## "Texas Flood"

Who thought that Texas could be flooded?
Isn't it all desert?

People can die of thirst
But surely not because of too much water

Little do people know
All over the USA

Dangers of flood that loom over Texas
Waters from rains

Hurricanes
All kinds of storms

Can bring swift destruction
To the Lone Star State

Lest they be brave
And obedient to the Divine call

To fulfil their prophetic obligations
That they have ignored

Refusing to advance the Kingdom of Christ
Christ's honor and His cause

As the Heavenly Hosts
The LORD of the Heavenly Armies

Wave from Heaven
They have no spiritual insight to see them

The floodgates of heaven opened up suddenly
Reminding them of the Heavenly power

The blessing and the destruction
That belongs to the LORD Jesus Christ

**"The Abyss"**

The chasm that separated the two worlds
In a seemingly endless abyss
So close yet so far
So near yet so invisible

They revolved in their own worlds
But somehow
The concentric circles did not meet often
And the common space went AWOL

And they walked
Thought and spoke
In worlds that did not find
A common ground

Only a slight passing
Like an invisible mist passing through
Or a fog appearing from nowhere
And everywhere but done so soon

The abyss in a parallel universe
The world that doesn't really exist
Except as the sum of vapidity
The gulf that separates the two worlds

H. C. Kim

## "The Alpha"

She searched for her Alpha
In all the wrong places
Maybe he will be my Alpha
Or a type of my Alpha

She decided to put him on
Like she does her stocking
With a run beneath her right foot
On the bottom sole

Then she tried another
For this one did not quite fit
No, he's not my Alpha
Or a type of my Alpha

She began to talk to herself
In her thoughts
In her dreams
And everyday became unreal

She wanted to numb the pain
And find her Alpha
Or a type of her Alpha
To make everything okay again

She felt like Eve
Who was thrust out of the Garden
Why did I listen to the Serpent?
She cried in her heart

Now, she felt only longing
Sadness coupled with a feeling of lack
A feeling of want

That cannot be satisfied

But she looked in all the wrong places
And hoped to realize her dream
Like chess pieces
Her brilliant mind did move

But she realized
She was the biggest piece on the board
In fact all was constant
And she only suffered deep inside

## "The Appetizer"

I am only the appetizer
And my sole purpose
Is to please and pleasure
Your taste buds
To make your meal experience complete

Why such long faces?
Bitterness
Sour expression
You are supposed to smile as you eat me
Them are the rules, don't you know?

Maybe the guy doesn't know the rules
Maybe the gal has forgotten them
But they look like sour puss
Black cat in the middle of a dog-ridden ally
A dog without a human friend

Just eat me
And get over it
Let me complete my mission
As the appetizer on your table
I exist to bring joy

Don't prolong my misery
With your frowns
And not even a single complement
About how I look
Or taste

Just put me out of my misery
Why don't you
Eat me

And get it over with
Let me fulfill my destiny

## "The Body Clock"

I thought about her
And felt that I missed her
For some reason
I felt a crawling nervousness
Like I had missed my plane

I wondered about her
Was there something
That my body clock tried to tell me?
Did my body know
What my mind did not?

## "The Crusader"

He just killed a Jew
His one year old baby
And the pregnant wife
A soldier of the Crusades

Why did you kill?
Asked a shocked Jew
Wearing a cross
To conceal his identity

The Crusader answered
We are in a Holy War
We follow the Old Testament
The War of Joshua

Did not Jesus taught love?
Asked the Jew in disguise
He taught to love the enemy
Love the neighbor as yourself

Jesus commanded
Destruction of Jerusalem
And the death of the Jews
In the New Testament

The Christian soldier continued
We are merely obeying his command
The Holy Word of God
And we fight to kill Jews and destroy Jerusalem

We will carry out a war
Worthy of the Name of Jesus
And the prophecy of the New Testament

That Jews must die and Jerusalem destroyed

The despondent Jew looked
Trying to persuade the Christian soldier
But decided to convert instead
To become a Christian himself

## "The Doughnut Pact"


The mayor won't like it at all
The partner said
Well he's one of them
He heard his partner say

I wonder if he counts
But I wouldn't try
It's a challenge
You like challenges, I know

Keep it simple, man
Okay, I guess you are right
We can be invisible
Sure we can, we are New York's finest

So, what we do is to give the doughnuts
Yes
To complete strangers
Yes

But how will we know it's one of them
Well, we are in the city, aren't we?
That don't mean nothing
Well, we'll ask

What?
We'll ask before giving the doughnuts
So, you and I will just give the doughnuts?
Yeah, why not?

So the plan is to walk up and give the doughnuts
Yes
You want to try with the mayor?

I have to confess I like him too much

To give the doughnuts?
Well, they are bad doughnuts
Yeah
No reason to risk things

Okay, so we give the doughnuts
One from me and one from you
To the same person
No, numskull, to two different people

At the same time?
No, don't have to be
Okay, let's call this The Doughnut Pact
That's the first smart thing you said

## "The Draw"

She drew a line
And it told a whole story
Of her pain
Resentment
And desires

I stared at the line
The contour of a sofa
The line even showed
The place where someone sat
Or lay

I could not help but to cry
At the power of the line
Drawn on a simple white canvas
A line fraught with the passions
Of a heart longing for something

Who could have thought
That a line could be so moving?
To tell a life's story
One's heart's desire
And the love lost

But the line was more than that
Much more than a story of a person
But a testimony of affection
A gift of protection
For the Beloved

## "The Drive"

The drive seemed so long and far
And she felt so very tired
Like the repetition of the sun
In Los Angeles
During the year
Was the drive that was endless

She wanted to give up
Because it went on and on
Without seeming end
She felt her fuel spent
And energy gone
She almost wanted to give in

Without questions
Without protests
Just to step outside
Of the car that drove on and on
And stand her feet
On solid ground

For all her love of excitement
And adventure
This was more than she had bargained for
And the joy of the prize however great
Seemed so far away
Refills after refills needed

She just did not feel
That she had the strength
To go on and on and on
She just wanted to stop her car
Get a cool glass of Cool Aid

And relax her toes

The drive has been so long
And who knows how far it would go?
But the pit stop was just around the corner
It would just be easy to stop
And rest awhile
For a long while

She tried to convince herself
That the destination mattered not really
But that she was where she should be
A pit stop that would give her respite
A pause and a type of a vacation
Even if from her dream

Little did she realize
That her goal was just 5 minutes away
But she stopped
5 minutes short of her goal
Never to know the joy of victory
And a hero's welcome that awaited her

**H. C. Kim**

## "The Fire Fighter"


The fire fighter did not know
That his own wife would die by fire
He was a fire fighter
For God's sakes!

He smiled uncontrollably
For he found the irony
Of the Divine Providence
In his wife's death

Through the tears
That marred his face
The uncontrollable shaking
That was so uncharacteristic

The big fire fighter cried
And smiled
Like a madman
Who lost everything

He had his friends in the department
And he had his mom and dad
And sisters and brothers
He was from a grand Irish Catholic family

But he did not think he had life
Until he found it in the love of his wife
She was everything to him
And she lay there, crisp and cooked

Dead as can be
Because of a fire
That swept through the building

She was hardly identifiable

He thought to himself
He now had to live a life on earth
Which has become a Hell for him
And in the madness of the moment

He jumped to his death
To join his dead Jewish wife
In Hell
But he only broke one leg

And limped around
As people watched
For God did not see it fit
For him to escape his Hell on earth

## "The Fuzzball"

The Fuzzball sits there
On top of the circular box
With Christmas trees drawn
All over its green surface

The Fuzzball is a penguin
With a wide white stomach
And the black tuxedo suit
But with yellow beak and feet

The Fuzzball has dazed eyeballs
Stuck on his stuffed body
And a pink scarf around his neck
Pink is his favorite color, you see

The Fuzzball is a cuddly plush doll
With a rice filled bottom
So pet-able
That the young maiden can't resist

The Fuzzball bounces
In all is fluffy fuzziness
Its small bottom
Filling her whole hand

## "The Great Fire"

The Great Fire rose
From the heart of the city
Certainly unexpected
So many already dead

But the fire would not stop
But raged on
It had already consumed
10 fire fighters

The Great Fire raged
And put the fear of God
In the hearts of all
In the city bearing the State name

The innocent died
Old and young
Healthy and sick
Handicapped and retarded too

The Great Fire advanced
Swallowing up one after another
The number of the dead rose
Fire fighters and civilians

Everyone is a target
In this war
Waged
With purifying fire

The Great Fire killed
Sent some to Heaven
And others to Hell

A few in the building survived

Why did not the fire fighters obey?
The civilians asked
This fire could have been prevented
In the first place

The people in tears
Blamed the fire fighters
For refusing to obey God
And give Him their service

## "The Wait"

She told herself
The wait was too long
For her heart had grown weary
From longing and hoping
She wanted to be near him

The more she saw him
She felt the wait
An undue punishment
That her existence had become futile
And the wait the greatest of life's curses

Then those who surrounded her
By wicked design and evil purpose
Convinced her
Like the Serpent in the Garden of Eden
That she could eat of the forbidden fruit

The fruit of the tree of the knowledge
Of good and evil
Will open your eyes
And you will see like God
Finding what you desire

So she partook
Of the fruit
The forbidden one
Because she could not overcome her doubts
She could not wait any longer

When she took the fruit
Took a bite
She knew that she was naked

And that she had taken a wrong step
But it was too late

She did not want to be alone
In her state of the knowledge of what happened
So she took the fruit
To give it to others
So that they can share in her pain

In her guilt
In her knowledge
Of good and evil
And feel the same pain
The emptiness afterwards

## "The Waited"

The lover waited
Having learned the customs
The language
And the ways
Of the Beloved

Yet came not
Reciprocity
Nor love
Even an ounce of caring
But only rejection

Violence perpetrated
Hatred filled disservice
Conniving plot
To strip away the honor
Dignity and human decency

The lover waited
For the cold heart to change
Year after year
He believed that
The Beloved will relent

But like madcow disease
The infestation hung on
And the plotting became worse
Like a chapter
Out of Dangerous Liaisons

Who knows what she suffered
In the past
By those who were unfair

Or maybe she imagined it all
But the Land remained adamant

Like a hardened stone
Persecuting mercilessly
As if that were a sign of love
To hurt and to maim
The Waited

## "The Yellow Cord"

The yellow cord
Weaved through the air
On a disk
Clothed in plastic
Sitting on top of a rectangle
Slanted North
Toward the thin crevice
Just underneath the leg
Of a top shelf
Teasing its way down
But abstaining from touch
In the back is the leg
That stretched down
Past the main layer
All the way down
To the ground
Made of wood
Years and years
Of memories it doth contain
Who can tell what was
Or what will be
On the wooden ground
Which squeaks sometimes
With an awkward step
Or a clumsy leaning
Armchair color
To match the table
Black next to black
Broken only by the
Skyblue disk
Sheathed in plastic
Lying on top of the rectangle
Reaching toward the thin crevice

Just underneath the leg
Of a top shelf

## "There is No Forgiveness"

Absolutely no forgiveness
For those who are not repentant
God will not forgive
Those who refuse to repent
Persisting in their evil ways

The LORD Jesus is God
Of the Old Testament
As well as the New
The Triune God
Existent from everlasting

Those who do not want
To submit to the will of Christ
God the Son
And God the Father
God the Holy Spirit

There is no forgiveness
Absolutely not
For the LORD will not forgive
Those who are not sorry
But continue in their evil ruse

The LORD is God
And the fear of the LORD
Is beginning of wisdom
The judgment shall come
To those who persist

## "Time Limit"

There was a time limit for her love
The expiration date
By which the milk will go sour
Never to be drunk again
But to be dumped down the drain

A love so passionate and real
But constrained and chained
By the forces of time
And their limitations
That enslaved her very fiber

Love does not conquer all
She told herself
And looked at the mirror
That stood before her
And noticed the clock going backwards

Time does not stand still
It moves
Forward mostly
But backwards
Relative to who you are

And she realized
The midnight hour was upon her
The joy of her life
On a balance
On a clock that was reflected by the mirror

She wondered
What she should do
To be resigned to Fate

Or to make her own destiny
Within the limitation that is Time

## "Tissue Paper"

Tissue paper lay there on the table
And I knew not what the story was
Was it a vestige of love lost
Or heartfelt joyful tears
Of love regained and triumphant?

Maybe the tissue lay there
Unused and brand new
Seeking only to be taken up
To be needed
To bring comfort

The tissue just sat there
Without any movement
With no indication
Telling no story
In its effeminate mystery

And I wondered
If I was reading too much
Into the story of the tissue
That just lay there
On top of my table

## "Tomorrow May Never Come"

Tomorrow may never come
I heard her say
And knew not whether
It was an entreaty of a threat

Love me now
Or forever lose my love
Those are my conditions
And the only choice you have

Or was it a heart of longing
Seeking realization
Right now and here
Prompting her love to act

For like a turtle
Slow and steady
But without any impulsive
Decision

She thought?
Who knows?
I guess I will never know
Unless she reveals it to me

## "Tough"


I am tough
I have taken a few bullets
Have lent my body as a shield
For my partner
Out of a sense of duty

I signed up to be NYPD
Because I wanted to be a hero
To the weak and the disenfranchised
And I fought with my life
For their safety

I am tough
I have scars to prove it
Record of risking my life
And all the dangers I took on
Without a second's thought

But I am not too tough
For I can't bear to see
My wife die
Before her time
Leaving me behind

That would destroy me
And my whole world
My reason for being
Purpose in life
I am not a religious man

But I believe in love
Her love
That has given me my meaning

A machine with a purpose
Turned into a human being by her hands

I am not so tough
I can't bear to see my wife die
I am not religious
But pray every day
That God will take me before her

What would I do
If she were gone?
Having tasted her love
There is no more reality left for me
But with her in it

I am not tough at all
Because I believe in the prophecy
I am not a religious man
Not even baptized
Don't go to church

But I believe in the prophecy
It is by faith I believe
And know that my religion is my wife
And she will be taken away
Destroying my world, my religion

I believe in the prophecy
And I know my wife is marked
But I am not tough at all
Because I cannot follow the prophecy
And doom myself to destruction

## "Uneasy"

They felt uneasy
As they closed the airplane door
Behind them
Ready to take off
Into the skies

It wasn't like they were afraid
Of flying high above the ground
They were used to it
It was their work
Daily they rode the plane

But this time
It was different
For some reason
They felt a pang of conscience
And fear that gripped them

Will this be the plane that crashes?
And claims their lives
The crew and the passengers
They felt guilt in their guts
And thought of the wrongs

They knew they should not have
But they did
And they knew that
Were there God
He would not look the other way

They closed the door
Even the atheist among them afraid
What if?

The plane taxied on the run way
Ready to take off onto the unknown skies

H. C. Kim

## "What If"

What if?
My partner asked
As we strolled down
Madison Avenue

What if?
What if what?
What if it's true?
What?

You know
What?
You know!
Okay

What if?
I don't know
Don't know what?
I just don't know

So you are not sure either
What do you think?
Yes, I know what you mean
So, what should we do?

We can work together
What? You crazy?
What if, tough?
Okay, I'm listening

It's just between you and me
Okay, mum is the word
We can work together

Yeah?

And make an insurance policy
Insurance policy?
Yeah, an insurance policy
I see what you mean

It just takes two between us, right?
Yeah
And we've done it before
That is right

Well, we are doing it for a good cause
What?
For our families
I see

Insurance is important right?
I guess so
Company insurance protects the family right?
Yeah

Well, this insurance is more important
The word you use!
Call a spade a spade
Yeah, I guess insurance policy works

You see, we work together
Okay
In a pact between partners
Yeah, I'm listening

And carry it out on two undeserving from them
What do you mean?
We can find a couple who deserve what's coming to them
I see what you mean

And then we just don't talk about it ever
Okay
One time thing
I guess that would be okay

## "Wounded Eagle"

She looked down at the wounded eagle
With a fierce beak still intact
Eyes piercing as ever
But with wincing pain
And a wounded pride

She stared at the strong wings
Which imbue birds of prey with fear
And the reputation of violence
That still lingers even in the wounded state
But there was something helpless

Her heart went out to the eagle
Whom she once stared with scorn and contempt
As a bird not prone to peace or friendship
But a violent predator
Wanting only to kill and destroy

She saw something in the now-frail bird
Inspiring her heart of mercy
Needing her love
And she felt a need to reach out
And pour her love to make him whole

## "Youth Spirit"

The youth spirit evaporated
Why?
He was not sure
Whether it was because he was pushed

He felt pushed
Boxed in
Trapped
Unlike a few weeks ago

He felt free
Alive
Liberated
And the master of his own destiny

But now
He felt it going
Youth Spirit
He always carried in his visage

And he walked
Like a lamb to the slaughter
Wherever he went
Not being sure of anything

He felt like a pawn
Having to play his part
In this rotten game
He did not want to participate in

He stumbled into it somehow
He could not even remember how
It seems like a distant memory

He thought to himself

But he picked up the game plan
As he was expected to do
Resigned to his fate
Now marking his path

# About the Poet

H. C. Kim is a Korean-American poet who constantly writes. He has written many books of poetry, including *Transitions: Poems* and *Unconditional Election: Poems*. He has lived and written poems all over the world – Korea, Israel, India, England, Germany, and the United States of America. Currently, H. C. Kim resides in New Jersey, "the Garden State."